On the second day of Christmas my true love gave to me,

two turtle doves

and a partridge in a pear tree.

KU-256-479

On the third day of Christmas
my true love gave to me,

three French hens,

two turtle doves
and a partridge in
a pear tree.

On the fourth day of Christmas
my true love gave to me,

four calling birds,

three French hens,
two turtle doves
and a partridge in
a pear tree.

On the fifth day of Christmas
my true love gave to me,

five gold rings,

four calling birds, three French hens,
two turtle doves and
a partridge in a pear tree.

On the sixth day of Christmas
my true love gave to me,

six geese a-laying,

five gold rings, four calling birds,
three French hens, two turtle doves
and a partridge in a pear tree.

On the **Seventh** day of Christmas
my true love gave to me,

**Seven swans
a-swimming,**

Six geese a-laying, five gold rings,
four calling birds, three French hens,
two turtle doves and
a partridge in a pear tree.

seven swans a-swimming,
six geese a-laying,
five gold rings, four calling birds,
three French hens, two turtle doves
and a partridge in a pear tree.

On the tenth day of Christmas
my true love gave to me,
ten lords
a-leaping,

nine ladies dancing,
eight maids a-milking,

seven swans a-swimming,
six geese a-laying,
five gold rings, four calling birds,
three French hens, two turtle doves
and a partridge in a pear tree.

eight maids a-milking, seven swans a-swimming,
six geese a-laying, five gold rings,
four calling birds, three French hens,
two turtle doves and a partridge in a pear tree.

Six geese a-laying, five gold rings, four calling birds,
three French hens, two turtle doves
and a partridge in a pear tree.